BEYOND THE THEORY: SCIENCE OF THE FUTURE

WHAT'S INSIDE A BLACK HOLE?

THEORIES ABOUT SPACE PHENOMENA

Tom Jackson

Gareth Stevens
PUBLISHING

Please visit our website, www.garethstevens.com.
For a free color catalog of all our high-quality books,
call toll free 1-800-542-2595 of fax 1-877-542-2596.

Cataloging-in-Publication Data

Names: Jackson, Tom.
Title: What's inside a black hole? theories about space phenomena / Tom Jackson.
Description: New York : Gareth Stevens Publishing, 2019. | Series: Beyond the theory: science of the future |
Includes glossary and index.
Identifiers: LCCN ISBN 9781538226681 (pbk.) | ISBN 9781538226674 (library bound)
Subjects: LCSH: Black holes (Astronomy)--Juvenile literature. | Astronomy--Juvenile literature.
Classification: LCC QB843.B55 J33 2019 | DDC 523.8'875--dc23

First Edition

Published in 2019 by
Gareth Stevens Publishing
111 East 14th Street, Suite 349
New York, NY 10003

© 2019 Gareth Stevens Publishing

Produced for Gareth Stevens by Calcium
Editors: Sarah Eason and Tim Cooke
Designers: Emma DeBanks and Lynne Lennon
Picture researcher: Rachel Blount

Picture credits: Cover: Shutterstock: Vadim Sadovski: foreground; Wikimedia Commons: Chandra X-ray
Observatory Center: background; Inside: Chandra X-ray Observatory: X-ray: NASA/CXC/ISDC/L.Pavan et al,
Radio: CSIRO/ATNF/ATCA Optical: 2MASS/UMass/IPAC-Caltech/NASA/NSF: p. 13; X-ray: NASA/CXC/ITA/
INAF/J.Merten et al, Lensing: NASA/STScI; NAOJ/Subaru; ESO/VLT, Optical: NASA/STScI/R.Dupke: p. 21;
X-ray: X-ray: NASA/CXC/NCSU/K.Borkowski et al; Optical: DSS: p. 10b; NASA/CXC/Penn State/B.Luo et al:
pp. 22-23; X-ray: NASA/CXC/SAO/E.Bulbul, et al: p. 20; X-ray: NASA/CXC/UCLA/Z.Li et al; Radio: NRAO/VLA:
pp. 14-15; X-ray: NASA/CXC/Univ of Michigan/R.C.Reis et al; Optical: NASA/STScI: p. 17t; NASA/GSFC/M.
Corcoran et al: p. 16; NASA: pp. 25, 31, 39t; 2MASS, T. H. Jarrett, J. Carpenter, & R. Hurt: p. 40; Jacob Bers
(Bersonic): pp. 5, 42-43b; High-Z Supernova Search Team, HST, NASA: pp. 36-37; NASA/ESA: p. 24; ESA/
Herschel/PACS/SPIRE/J. Fritz, U. Gent; X-ray: ESA/XMM Newton/EPIC/W. Pietsch, MPE: p. 28b; NASA, ESA, M.J.
Jee and H. Ford (Johns Hopkins University): p. 30; NASA's Goddard Space Flight Center: pp. 1, 6-7; Hubble
Heritage Team (STScI/AURA), NASA: p. 26b; NASA/JPL-CalTech: pp. 8-9; NASA/JPL-Caltech/GSFC: p. 39cr;
Dave Lane: p. 4; MPE/GROND: p. 41; X-ray: NASA/CXC/Univ. of Alabama/A. Morandi et al; Optical: SDSS,
NASA/STScI: p. 35; Shutterstock: Vadim Sadovski: p. 34; Wikimedia Commons: Chandra X-ray Observatory
Center: p. 10–11; ESA/Hubble: pp. 26-27; European Space Agency & NASA: pp. 8-9; NASA, N. Benitez
(JHU), T. Broadhurst (Racah Institute of Physics/The Hebrew University), H. Ford (JHU), M. Clampin (STScI),
G. Hartig (STScI), G. Illingworth (UCO/Lick Observatory), the ACS Science Team and ESA: pp. 28-29; Ken
Spencer: p. 33t; Amber Stuver: p. 43c; Photograph by Orren Jack Turner, Princeton, N.J.: p. 22c.

Printed in the United States of America

CPSIA compliance information: Batch #CS18GS:
For further information contact Gareth Stevens, New York, New York at 1-800-542-2595.

CONTENTS

CHAPTER 1

SPACE
PHENOMENA

Astronomy, or the study of space, is probably the oldest science of all. With few lights at night, early humans had an excellent view of the starry sky.

Early peoples saw many things they could not explain, but they also noticed patterns among the points of light. Cave paintings from 30,000 years ago show groups of stars. Ancient **astronomers** from Egypt, Babylon, China, and Greece watched as these patterns, or **constellations**, moved through the sky. Most of the patterns seemed to be fixed, but a few lights moved along their own paths. The Greeks called them *planetai*, or "wanderers." We know them as **planets**.

Today, we can still clearly see the stars in the sky at night in places where there are no artificial lights.

Distant galaxies may have giant black holes at their centers.

Early astronomers were able to learn a lot about planets simply by looking at them. They figured out how the planets move around the sun, how large and heavy they are, and what they are made from. Modern astronomers study distant stars in the same way—they watch how they behave.

Today, our map of the sky is a lot more detailed than in the past. The latest maps contain the location of 48 million (4.8×10^7) objects. These are probably just the brightest ones. Astronomers estimate there are at least 10^{24} stars in the universe. However, not everything we see is a star. Astronomers have discovered space rocks such as meteors, asteroids, and long-tailed comets, which are balls of ice and dust. There are huge gas clouds called nebulae, and spiral swarms of billions of stars, known as galaxies.

But we cannot see the strangest space objects at all. They are so dark they are called black holes. In fact, most of space is made up of mysterious invisible **phenomena**, such as black holes, dark **matter**, and dark energy. Explaining these phenomena is at the cutting edge of modern astronomy. To learn more about them, it is necessary to go beyond the theory.

WHAT ARE
BLACK HOLES?

A black hole is an object in space that is many times the weight of the sun. A black hole has a mass that is at least eight times greater than that of the sun. In comparison with other stars, our sun is relatively small, but it is still more than 100 times larger than Earth. That gives an idea of the enormous amount of matter involved in black holes. However, although black holes have many times more mass than Earth, they are far, far smaller. In fact, all the material in a black hole is compressed, or squashed, into a single point in space!

Astronomers call the space filled by a black hole a singularity. It is so tiny that it has no length or width—and the matter within it is infinitely, or endlessly, dense. The laws of physics that scientists use to explain the behavior of the rest of the universe, from whole galaxies to tiny **particles** such as **atoms**, do not apply inside the singularity. That is another way of saying that astronomers do not really know what is going on inside a black hole—not yet, anyway. It is not certain that they ever will.

UNANSWERED

A black hole gives out no light and no material—and so it also gives out no information for astronomers trying to study it. It is simply a hole in space. No one has ever seen a black hole, and no one ever will. There is nothing to see. However, astronomers can predict what effects a black hole would have on the space around it. They use these clues to pinpoint the location of possible black holes.

black hole

star dust

In this illustration, a black hole pulls a passing star to shreds, then blows pieces of it back into space.

The pull of **gravity** created by a singularity is so huge that nothing can escape it. Its escape velocity—the speed an object has to travel to break free of another object's gravity—is faster than the **speed of light**. Nothing with mass can reach the speed of light, so it could never escape from the pull of a black hole.

OVER THE
HORIZON

In 1916, the great physicist Albert Einstein wrote a brilliant theory called *General Theory of Relativity*. His theory made it possible to describe what a black hole is like. General relativity explains the universe in a strange way.

Einstein did not describe a universe in which stars, planets, and other lumps of mass move around in space, pulling on one another or smashing together. Instead, he described everything in terms of energy bending space.

The outer limit of a black hole is called the event horizon. This is an imaginary line around the black hole where the gravitational pull gets powerful enough to stop light. If you cross the event horizon, you can never return to tell your tale—even if you could survive the experience. Arriving feet first at the event horizon, your feet would experience a much stronger pull of gravity than your head.

This is an artist's impression of a black hole. No one will ever know if it resembles the reality.

BEHIND THE THEORY

The existence of black holes was first proposed at the end of the 1700s. The French mathematician Simon Pierre Laplace called them "corps obscure," or "dark bodies." The term "black hole" was first used in 1958. The English physicist Stephen Hawking came up with a new way of thinking about black holes in the 1960s. Hawking showed that black holes followed the "big picture" rules of relativity but could also be described using the "small picture" theories of **quantum physics**. After all, a black hole is very big and very small at the same time.

The space around you would become ever more warped, and this would stretch your body hugely in a process called spaghettification. You will not be around to enjoy it! The forces would rip your body, your **cells**, and even your atoms to shreds.

A fellow astronaut watching you from a safe distance would see you approach the event horizon, and then grind to a halt. You would have entered space that is so curved that from someone else's point of view you would have ceased to move through time—and you would be locked in that position for eternity! No one would ever see what happens next.

FORMED FROM DYING STARS

Black holes are created in the biggest explosions in the universe. These events, known as supernovae, occur when the largest stars run out of fuel. Supernova means "big new." The explosion makes a new star appear in the sky, where it previously seemed there was nothing. In fact, the star was always there: it was just too dark to see before it exploded.

A star is a ball of plasma, or hot, electrified gas, that is collapsing under its own weight. The pressure at the center of this seething blob is so enormous that the atoms fuse, or join, together.

A black hole called Cygnus X-1 pulls in matter from a giant star and shoots out streams of dust.

This cloud of gas was created by the supernova G11 about 14,000 light-years away in Earth's galaxy, the Milky Way.

UNANSWERED

Our star is classed as an orange dwarf, meaning it is small and of medium temperature, so it will not die in a supernova. In about 5 billion years it will become cooler and swell into a red giant that will swallow Mercury and Venus—and perhaps Earth. Then the star will gradually drift apart, leaving a white-hot core about the size of Earth. This core will be a white dwarf. Astronomers think it will gradually cool, forming a cold, dark star called a black dwarf—but it will take a long time to find out for sure. It will take a trillion years for a white dwarf to cool that much, and that is 76 times longer than the current age of the universe.

Stars are mostly **hydrogen**, and two hydrogen atoms merge into one **helium** atom. When the hydrogen runs out, the helium atoms start to fuse, creating **elements** such as carbon and oxygen. (That means 90 percent of your atoms were made inside a star. The other 10 percent were made at the beginning of time—see page 26.)

Dwarf stars, which are relatively small stars like our sun, fizzle out after all the helium inside them is used up, but giant stars keep on fusing their atoms into heavier materials. Eventually, the star becomes so heavy it falls in on itself. The crush causes a final burst of **nuclear fusion** that makes the heaviest atoms of all, such as gold. Some of this new material is thrown off into space. This debris will one day form the rocks of a new **solar system**. But a giant star's collapse is so powerful that the rest of it falls in on itself and is compacted into a pinhead of super-dense, super-weird, and super-dark material—a black hole.

MESSAGES
FROM SPACE?

Our eyes see a narrow band of radiation as visible light, but the universe is full of other kinds of invisible radiation, such as radio waves, that work in the same way as light. Using these other kinds of radiation would not reveal black holes, but it might make it possible to find other nonvisible objects.

In 1967, British astronomers built a telescope to "see" space using radio waves. The telescope took the form of 4,000 pieces of wire hung in a field near Cambridge, England, like a clothes line. These wires picked up something very strange—a beep, beep of radio waves coming from a dark patch of sky.

The signal, named LGM-1, beeped every 1.3 seconds. Astronomers had found the first pulsar, or "pulsating star." A pulsar sends out a beam of radio waves that sweeps around as the star spins, like a lighthouse. But LGM-1 was spinning every 1.3 seconds! The sun takes 27 days to spin on its axis, so what kind of star spins so fast?

BEHIND THE THEORY

Pulsars were first found and described in the early 1970s by the British astronomer Jocelyn Bell Burnell. However, Burnell did not get the credit. Her bosses, two older men, received the acclaim and won awards for the discovery, including the 1974 Nobel Prize for Physics. Burnell did not let this stop her and continued to work to become one of Britain's leading astronomers.

A pulsar shoots a jet 37 light-years long into space.

This image of the Crab Nebula was mapped by using both visible and nonvisible radiation.

The answer is a neutron star. Some supernovae fail to become black holes. Instead the atoms from the dead star crush together and become a lump of pure **neutrons**. A neutron star is only about 12 miles (19.3 km) wide, but weighs about 1.5 times as much as the sun. Many more pulsars have been discovered, and it seems that LGM-1 is a slowpoke. The fastest pulsar spins 716 times every second!

CHAPTER 2

WHAT'S
OUT THERE?

How do you find something invisible, like a black hole? Astronomers think that the best place to start looking is close to home. The galaxy to which Earth's sun belongs is called the Milky Way. It is a spiral disk containing about 100 billion stars and swirls around in its own patch of space. On clear nights, the heart of the galaxy appears as a pale band of stars across the middle of the sky. The ancient Greeks called the pale glow caused by the combined light of these packed stars the *galaxías kýklos*, or "milk circle." That later became the Milky Road, then Milky Path, and now Milky Way. The word *galaxy*, meanwhile, comes from the Greek word for milk.

The central point of the Milky Way lies in the constellation of Sagittarius. There is no star at that location visible to the naked eye, but astronomers using radio telescopes have discovered a region of dust and gases there that gives out a powerful blast of radio waves. This object is known as Sagittarius A*, pronounced "A star."

Dust blocks the view of Sagittarius A* from Earth, but astronomers measured the motion of the stars nearby. This gave them an idea of how heavy the object was—and it was very heavy. In the later 1990s, the American astronomer Andrea Ghez found a way of detecting heat coming from inside the dust cloud at the heart of the galaxy, enabling her to find stars even closer to Sagittarius A*. The stars were orbiting the central object, and those closest to it were traveling at a quarter of the speed of light—that is nearly 2,000 times faster than our own solar system is moving through space.

Sagittarius A* was also giving out huge blasts of X-rays. Astronomers figured out that these were caused by gas and dust heating up as they are sucked into a black hole that lies at the heart of our own galaxy.

This view of Sagittarius A* shows a shock wave (blue) where energy blasted out of the black hole hit gas a few light-years away.

QUASARS AND BLAZARS

Earth's local black hole, Sagittarius A*, weighs 4 million times more than the sun. Astronomers describe it as being supermassive. As it spins, it twists the space—and time—around it into a corkscrew. Anything that comes within about 7.4 million miles (12 million km) and crosses its event horizon is sucked in and adds extra weight. So will Earth's solar system be sucked in one day?

The answer is probably no. The black hole grew large by eating up stars when the galaxy was young, but it swept the space around it clean long ago. Perhaps the black hole was there before the galaxy formed. To find out, astronomers are looking back in time to find a young galaxy being eaten by a black hole.

To astronomers, distance and time are the same thing. Light comes from stars at the speed of light, and the distance light travels in a year is called a light-year.

Intense X-ray activity (red and blue) marks an area of star formation in the Milky Way.

When we look at a star 10 light-years away, we see what it looked like 10 years ago. If we look 12 billion light-years away, we see the brightest objects in the universe. Each of these objects gives out 100 times more light than the whole Milky Way. Astronomers call them quasars, short for "quasi-stellar radio sources."

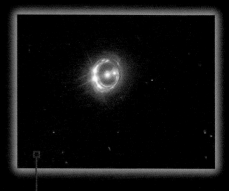

RX J1131 is a quasar about 6 billion light-years from Earth.

A quasar is an active **nucleus** of a galaxy, where a supermassive black hole is eating up millions of stars. The spinning black hole creates a jet of radiation, which is what is visible from Earth. If the jet is pointing straight in our direction, the galaxy appears super bright and is called a blazar. One blazar—S5 0014+81—is 25,000 times brighter than the Milky Way. Its black hole is 40 billion times heavier than the sun, with an event horizon that covers an area larger than our solar system.

UNANSWERED

Stephen Hawking suggested the revolutionary idea that black holes slowly **evaporate**. Hawking's idea is that the way the tiniest particles and **subparticles** behave at the event horizon—their quantum behavior—means that energy slowly leaks out of black holes. Given enough time, black holes will all disappear in a flash of **gamma rays**. The Fermi Space Telescope in orbit around Earth is looking for these flashes. So far, it has seen nothing.

OUR PLACE IN THE UNIVERSE

For most of history, people assumed Earth was the center of the universe and that everything else moved around it. In 1543, the Polish astronomer Nicolaus Copernicus showed that Earth moved around the sun, but astronomers still put the solar system at the heart of the universe. As telescopes got better, however, astronomers began to see fuzzy clouds and spirals and disks of light in space. In 1929, American Edwin Hubble showed that these were other galaxies, separated from the Milky Way by huge distances. The sun was on the outer edge of the Milky Way, which was itself not a very spectacular galaxy. It is not even the biggest galaxy in the local neighborhood.

M101 is a spiral galaxy like our own. It is 21 million light-years from Earth.

BEHIND THE THEORY

Measuring the distances to the stars is difficult. A hot giant star far away looks the same as a closer cool dwarf star. In 1908, US astronomer Henrietta Swan Leavitt was investigating Cepheid variables. These stars change in brightness in a regular rhythm matching the star's size and brightness. Leavitt used this fact to figure out how far away they were. In 1929, Edwin Hubble showed that Cepheid variables in the Milky Way were much closer to Earth than those in other galaxies. The universe got a lot bigger.

The Milky Way is a spiral galaxy in which the stars are arranged in a rotating disk and have bunched up into arms that sweep out from a central bulge. Younger disk galaxies have yet to develop these spiral arms.

The latest surveys suggest that there are 2 trillion galaxies in the universe, each with billions of stars. Astronomers have identified thousands of "exoplanets" around other stars (an exoplanet is any planet outside the solar system). It is probable that there are more planets than stars, and even if **habitable** plants like Earth are really rare, there would still be billions of them—more than there are grains of sand on all of Earth's beaches.

SUPERSTRUCTURE
OF THE UNIVERSE

Fo generations, astronomers on Earth have picked out patterns among the stars to create constellations such as Cassiopeia, Pegasus, and the Southern Cross. However, at a great distance from Earth, we would struggle to see those shapes. Although the stars would be in the same place, they would form new patterns. Therefore, an accurate map of the universe would have to be three-dimensional, and for the last 20 years, the Sloane Digital Sky Survey (SDSS) has been producing just such a map.

This cluster of galaxies lies in the constellation of Perseus.

The Sky Survey has not mapped the billions of individual stars. Instead, it has mapped about 900,000 of the brightest galaxies and quasars. The map shows that our galaxy and 53 others form a cluster called the Local Group. In turn, the gravity of the Local Group and hundreds of other clusters forms the Laniakea Supercluster, which is 250 million light-years wide.

Astronomers believed that superclusters were the biggest things in the universe. However, the SDSS has revealed that superclusters line up in "great walls" a billion light-years long. Everything we see lies inside a tangled network of these walls, which surround huge voids. The universe is mostly empty.

The red and blue areas of this image may show the collision of four galaxy clusters.

UNANSWERED

Astronomers believe the voids between the great walls of the universe are too big. There is not enough matter in the universe and there has not been enough time in history for gravity to have created all the voids that exist. One explanation is cosmic inflation. This theory says that in the first moments of the universe, space inflated remarkably quickly. As it did so, tiny changes in energy appeared in the otherwise completely empty universe. All matter—the stars, planets, and even humans—formed in these wrinkled regions.

CHAPTER 3

EXPANDING SPACE

The first person to fully explain how the moon, the planets, and the rest of our solar system were all moving was Isaac Newton. In the seventeenth century, Newton figured out laws of motion and gravity to describe a universe in which everything moved in circles and nothing ever really changed. According to Newton, the universe worked like a huge piece of perfect clockwork.

About 250 years later, the idea of this clockwork universe no longer matched what scientists had discovered by working on atomic physics and mathematics. Albert Einstein came up with a new explanation. He suggested that the universe was "relativistic," meaning that it was always changing and could never be still.

Albert Einstein's predictions of the behavior of the universe have largely been proven in the century since he published them.

Einstein's suggestion led to another question: Is the universe getting bigger or smaller? The answer came from the color of starlight. Light is a wave, and behaves in the same way as other waves, such as ocean and sound waves. Most people have heard how the pitch of a police or fire siren changes as a vehicle rushes past. This phenomenon is called the Doppler Shift. The sound wave is squashed a little as the siren moves toward the listener, making it sound high-pitched. As the car starts moving away, the sound is stretched, making it sound lower.

The same thing happens to light waves. The light from stars moving toward us is compressed so it changes color. Those coming toward us appear more blue (called a blueshift), while stars moving away appear more red (called a redshift). When astronomers looked beyond our galaxy, they found that all the light was redshifted. Everything we can see is moving away from us—and fast. Where's it all going?

In some senses, the answer is that it's not going anywhere. The motion is due to the space between us and distant galaxies getting larger. The universe is expanding, so every object we see is getting farther away from us and from all other objects. Has space always expanded like this? Will the expansion continue? And what was space like in the past, when it was smaller?

This image from the Chandra Space Observatory is the deepest X-ray image ever of the farthest and oldest parts of the universe.

REWIND TO THE START

If the universe is expanding, it is obvious that it must have been smaller in the past. The age of the universe is called Hubble Time. It is calculated by looking at the current size of the universe now and how quickly it is expanding, and then figuring out how long it has taken to get that big. The most recent estimate for the age of the universe is about 13.8 billion years.

What was the universe like 13.8 billion years ago? In 1927, the French priest and physicist George Lemaître came up with a theory of how the universe was created. He called it the Cosmic Egg, but it was later renamed the Big Bang Theory. The Big Bang Theory says that the universe started from a single point in space, called a singularity. All the energy and space of the universe was in this point.

This image shows some of the oldest galaxies in the universe.

UNANSWERED

The three dimensions of space are lengthening all the time. The material in space is not getting bigger, but the space around it is. What emptiness is this growing space filling—if it is not just more space? The only answer that makes sense is that there is at least one more dimension, which physicists call hyperspace. Our universe is an expanding bubble inside hyperspace. However, scientists have yet to detect or measure any extra dimensions.

Physicists have not yet figured out what the singularity was like, but they have a good idea what happened after the Big Bang. Today, only the first 10^{-35} seconds (100 quadrillion quintillionths of a second) are a mystery. The universe likely doubled in size many hundreds of times, going from a billionth of the size of a **proton** to between the size of a marble and a grapefruit.

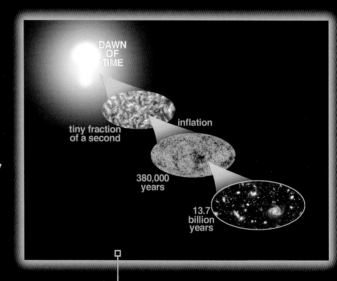

DAWN
OF
TIME

tiny fraction
of a second

inflation

380,000
years

13.7
billion
years

This young universe was very hot indeed, but cooled as it got steadily bigger—it is now very cold, at around −454°F (−270°C). As the universe cooled, pure energy separated into the units we call particles. These particles became the forces and matter that make the universe we see around us.

This NASA image shows how the universe took shape after the Big Bang.

STAR NURSERIES

It took hundreds of thousands of years for the universe to cool enough for atoms to form. Today, three-quarters of the atoms in the universe are hydrogen atoms, which are the smallest and simplest atoms. All these hydrogen atoms were formed during the Big Bang.

The first stars formed 100 million years or so after the Big Bang, from huge clouds of hydrogen. Today, astronomers study the formation of stars by looking into nebulae. Areas of the cloud with a little more dust in them reflect light, making one patch of gas slightly colder. The cool gas moves more slowly than hotter gases and reacts more to the forces of gravity, which pull it together. It forms a tighter and tighter—and darker—object, known as a globule.

Stars are born in dark regions known as Bok globules (top right).

BEHIND THE THEORY

In 1947, Bart and Priscilla Bok, a husband-and-wife team of astronomers who worked in the United States, studied the black clouds seen in space. They proposed that these dark nebulae were stellar nurseries, where new stars were forming. The phenomena were named Bok globules in their honor. Forty years later, the Chinese-American astronomer Frank Shu came up with the theory of how **protostars** formed inside the globules (see below).

These huge pillars of dust and gas mark areas of star formation.

Astronomers suggest that, over a period of 10 million years, a globule collapses into a tight core called a protostar. A protostar is cold but eventually grows big enough for nuclear fusion to begin as a small amount of deuterium, or "heavy hydrogen," burns away inside. The heat makes the surface of the star bubble, which creates magnetism. The **magnetic field** pushes out jets of hot gas from the star's north and south poles, which blast through the dust cloud around the star. These jets grow wider as the star warms up, spreading until the whole surface is giving out heat and light. The shroud of dust is finally pushed away to reveal the universe's newest star.

CHAPTER 4

MISSING MATTER

Astronomers, astrophysicists, and planetary scientists have been able to figure out the workings of the universe in great detail without ever leaving Earth. Telescopes of increasing accuracy are looking ever farther into space and seeing ever smaller objects. At the same time, probes continue to explore the weird alien worlds of our own solar system. However, one big mystery has remained unsolved for almost 50 years. Most of the universe is missing!

In the 1920s, astronomers found that our sun is part of a swirling spiral of stars called the Milky Way. They assumed that the solar system and all the other stars in the galaxy orbited a central point in the same way the planets **orbit** the sun. When they measured the speed of stars in these orbits, however, they found that they seemed to be going too fast to fit with the theory. The scientists decided that the results must be mistakes in measurements, and the field of investigation was largely dropped.

The galaxy Andromeda has stars that orbit incredibly quickly.

However, in 1979 an American researcher named Vera
Rubin returned to the subject and measured the rotation
of Andromeda, the nearest spiral galaxy to our own. Rubin
confirmed that the earlier results were correct: the spin was
too fast to match the theory. Rubin was able to estimate the
mass of Andromeda from the light its stars produced, but
a galaxy that size spinning as quickly as Andromeda would
be flinging out stars due to centrifugal force, the force that
throws water outward from a garden sprinkler.

The only answer was that Andromeda must have a lot more
gravity to hold it together than Rubin had calculated—and
therefore that it must weigh a lot more than is accounted for
by what we can see. It now appears that about 85 percent
of Andromeda is invisible, or dark, matter.

Dark matter is called dark because it is not affected by
electricity or magnetism at all, so it does not form atoms
or give out light or any other radiation. We know it is
everywhere—there is dark matter in our sun, in Earth,
even in humans—but scientists are still in the dark as to
what dark matter actually is.

WIMPS AND MACHOS

Scientists believe that there are four fundamental forces in the universe. The strong force holds atomic nuclei together. The weak force is involved in radioactivity, changing particles in the nucleus. The electromagnetic force holds electrons around the nucleus. Gravity is the weakest but widest-ranging force, acting across huge distances. Dark matter was discovered by detecting the effects of its gravity, but the other forces seem to have no impact on it.

There are two theories about what dark matter might be, known as MaCHOs and WIMPs. MaCHOs stands for Massive Compact Halo Objects. A halo is a dim region visible around galaxies, where astronomers think there may be many heavy (compact) objects. These objects include brown dwarfs, which are protostars that never quite got big enough to glow, and micro black holes. However, it is highly unlikely that galactic halos will add up to 85 percent of the known universe, which is how much dark matter astronomers believe exists.

A faint dark ring (highlighted) in a distant galaxy cluster might be evidence that dark matter exists in halos.

BEHIND THE THEORY

The term "dark matter" was first used by Fritz Zwicky, a Swiss-American astronomer who observed its effects in the 1930s but assumed that his observations were due to an error. Zwicky is also famous for discovering supernovae and for launching the first objects out of Earth's orbit in 1957. Although they were only small metal balls, these tiny "spacecraft" are still in orbit around the sun.

That leaves WIMPs, or Weakly Interacting Massive Particles. These particles move through space, through Earth—through anything—without causing any effects on normal matter. Because they are unnoticeable, finding WIMPs is difficult (assuming they even exist). The latest method being tried is to build huge tanks of supercooled **liquid xenon** in deep mines, where the detector is shielded from light and other ordinary particles. The idea is that very occasionally a WIMP will hit a xenon atom at just the right angle to make it emit a weak flicker of light, but so far nothing has been detected.

There is a third way to explain dark matter: perhaps our understanding of mass and gravity is just wrong.

CHAPTER 5

DARK
ENERGY

Astronomers might be getting closer to solving the mystery of dark matter, but there is an even bigger dark mystery to solve: dark energy. This is the name given to a kind of antigravity force that is pushing space apart. Ever since Edwin Hubble proved that all the galaxies in the universe were moving away from us and from one another, astronomers have wanted to measure the expansion of the universe more accurately.

The initial theory suggested that the universe is expanding because of the Big Bang, but gravity is acting like a brake on that expansion, slowing it down. Scientists wondered if there is enough gravity from all the stars and galaxies to eventually slow the expansion to a halt—and perhaps to make the universe shrink in the future. Or is the universe so lightweight that it will just drift apart forever?

In 1999, astronomers found a way to answer that question by measuring how much the expanding universe had stretched, or redshifted, the light of dozens of supernovae many billions of light-years away. They expected to discover that the light of older supernovae had been stretched more than the light of younger, nearer stars because the universe's expansion was slowing down.

Edwin Hubble used the 100-inch (254 cm) Hooker Telescope at the Mount Wilson Observatory in California to figure out that the universe is expanding.

Instead, scientists found that the expansion of the universe was getting faster and faster. Gravity made the expansion slow down a little after the Big Bang, but then a mysterious process made it speed up again. Around 3 billion years ago, this mysterious "dark energy" became the most powerful force in the universe.

The discovery of dark energy was one of the most profound in all of scientific history. Three-quarters of all the energy in the universe is dark energy, a fifth of the universe is dark matter, while the rest (about 4 percent) is the ordinary matter that is inside all the billions and billions of star systems across space. Today, astronomers know more than ever about the universe—but mostly they know that they do not yet understand how most of the universe works!

All the objects in this image of ultra-deep space are being sped up by a mysterious force.

END OF THE UNIVERSE

Many experts used to think that the universe would end in a reverse Big Bang called the Big Crunch. The expansion of space would slow and stop, and then gravity would begin to pull together the stars and galaxies again until they collapsed in a huge explosion.

The discovery of dark energy has changed how scientists think about the universe. Assuming that dark energy continues to dominate the universe—it might not, but no one knows—the universe will end in a Big Rip. This is estimated to happen in about 22 billion years. (Earth will already be gone, destroyed by the dying sun in 5 billion years).

Will the universe collapse in on itself in a "big crunch"?

ABELL 1835   MS 1455.0+2232

Dark energy grows stronger as space gets bigger, so eventually it will become more powerful than gravity and will pull galaxies apart. Stars will become further spread out from one another. Eventually the stars themselves will be ripped open and stop shining. Even atoms will be pulled apart, creating a soup of **electrons** and **quark particles** spread over a huge area.

Some scientists are working on theories that show that these super-cold, super-low-energy conditions are what caused the Big Bang. One theory says that the energy of the universe is zero, because all the matter energy is canceled out by the gravity energy, adding up to nothing at all. That is why a universe like ours could form from nothing at all.

UNANSWERED

Dark energy appears to come from nothing. In the early universe, there was no empty space, so there was no dark energy. After 10 million years, however, the universe had lots of space, so the energy of nothing, or **vacuum** energy, was enormous. Quantum physics explains that vacuums contain a possibility of energy, as **virtual** particles flicker into existence. Dark energy may be linked to the combined effect of each virtual particle in the vastness of space.

SEEING FARTHER

Astronomers believe that the answers to the mysteries of the universe are out there, and we just need bigger, better, or different telescopes to find them. This has been the way astronomers have worked for centuries. In the fifteenth century, Ulug Beg, the ruler of Samarkand in Central Asia, built a sextant that was three stories high. This huge tool could measure the position of stars and planets more accurately than ever. In the 1600s, Galileo built a telescope bigger than anyone before him, with a 9-inch (23 cm) lens. This revealed for the first time the moons of Jupiter, the way the appearance of Venus changes, and the mass of stars at the center of the Milky Way.

A supernova explodes at the edge of a spiral galaxy. Measuring the strength of such explosions reveals how far away they are—revealing to astronomers a far larger universe than they predicted.

Sixty years later, Isaac Newton invented a new telescope that used mirrors rather than glass lenses, meaning that much larger telescopes could be built. In 1845, the Irish amateur astronomer Lord Rosse built the Leviathan, a giant telescope with a mirror 71 inches (180 cm) across. This was powerful enough to make the first clear images of distant spiral galaxies.

In the 1990s astronomy went into space with the Hubble Space Telescope (HST). HST used a spy-satellite design, but its 94-inch (240 cm) mirror was pointed toward space. Although larger telescopes had been built on Earth, the air above them made stars appear blurry, so from its orbit above Earth, HST gave the clearest view of the stars ever seen. Its Ultra Deep Field image looked at a small patch of empty sky. In that tiny region, HST saw 10,000 galaxies that were up to 13.2 billion years old.

In 2024, the Extremely Large Telescope will start work on a mountain in Chile. Its main mirror will be 129 feet (3,930 cm) across! It will use computers to flex and adjust its mirrors to counteract the distortions of the atmosphere. Scientists hope that the ELT will be able to study the atmospheres of planets in distant solar systems—and perhaps to find evidence of alien life.

However, to see to the very edge of the universe, and to the moments after the Big Bang, will require an entirely new way of imaging space— one that uses gravity rather than light.

COSMIC MICROWAVE BACKGROUND

The farthest astronomers can see at the moment is about 13.4 billion light-years. This is when the first light was released into the universe. The time before that—the first 380,000 years of the universe—is called the Dark Ages. Energy and matter were so compressed in the early universe that light and other radiation could not shine out. As soon as one particle released radiation, another particle absorbed the radiation.

At the end of the Dark Ages, the universe cooled down enough for electrons to join with protons and neutrons to make the first atoms. As they gave up their energy and settled into position, the universe's electrons gave out a huge flash of light that appeared from all parts of the sky. The flash released 100 times more energy than that released from all of today's stars and galaxies combined. So why isn't the sky still lit up by this light?

Originally, the wavelength of ancient light—the distance between peaks in its ripples of energy—measured billionths of a meter, but it has been hugely stretched as light passes through expanding space. Now the wavelengths are measured in micrometers (millionths of a meter). That is not visible light but microwave radio radiation, which can only be "seen" with a radio receiver.

This phenomenon is called the Cosmic Microwave Background, or CMB. It is our best source of evidence for the Big Bang. However, what happened to the universe after the CMB event is still a mystery. To see that, astronomers are building the largest space telescope ever—and they will need to put it somewhere very dark and very cold.

This map of patterns of radiation shows the shape of the universe 13.7 billion years ago.

This image includes background light from the first billion years after the Big Bang.

UNANSWERED

Although the CMB signal is more or less the same everywhere, there are tiny differences, with parts being slightly hotter or colder than the rest. Every hot spot represents a place where a supercluster of galaxies later formed, and cold spots became empty voids. There is one very large cold spot in the CMB, known simply as the Cold Spot. The Cold Spot is probably now an empty space, known as the Eridanus Supervoid.

LOOKING FOR HEAT

Astronomers want to look at the first generation of stars to learn how galaxies formed. However, while the light from the CMB has been stretched into microwaves, the light from the first stars is not quite so old, so it has not been stretched as much. As a result, it is now **infrared** or heat radiation.

In the official map of a survey carried out by Harvard University, each dot represents a galaxy, color coded to show its redshift, or distance from Earth.

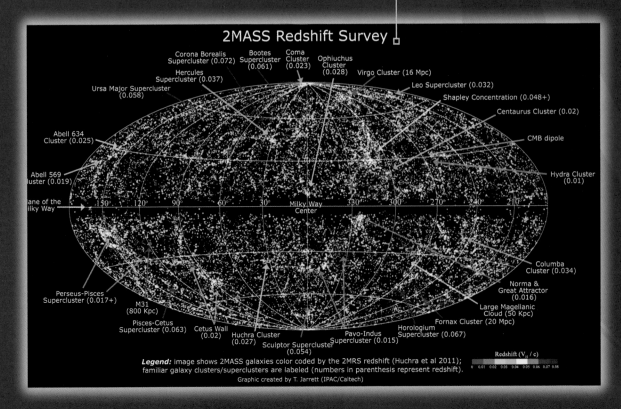

2MASS Redshift Survey

Corona Borealis Supercluster (0.072)
Bootes Supercluster (0.061)
Coma Cluster (0.023)
Ophiuchus Cluster (0.028)
Virgo Cluster (16 Mpc)
Hercules Supercluster (0.037)
Ursa Major Supercluster (0.058)
Leo Supercluster (0.032)
Shapley Concentration (0.048+)
Centaurus Cluster (0.02)
Abell 634 Cluster (0.025)
CMB dipole
Abell 569 Cluster (0.019)
Hydra Cluster (0.01)
Plane of the Milky Way
150° 120° 90° 60° 30° Milky Way Center 330° 300° 270° 240° 210°
Columba Cluster (0.034)
Perseus-Pisces Supercluster (0.017+)
Norma & Great Attractor (0.016)
M31 (800 Kpc)
Large Magellanic Cloud (50 Kpc)
Pisces-Cetus Supercluster (0.063)
Cetus Wall (0.02)
Huchra Cluster (0.027)
Sculptor Supercluster (0.054)
Pavo-Indus Supercluster (0.015)
Horologium Supercluster (0.067)
Fornax Cluster (20 Mpc)

Redshift (V_H / c)
0 0.01 0.02 0.03 0.04 0.05 0.06 0.07 0.08

Legend: image shows 2MASS galaxies color coded by the 2MRS redshift (Huchra et al 2011); familiar galaxy clusters/superclusters are labeled (numbers in parenthesis represent redshift).
Graphic created by T. Jarrett (IPAC/Caltech)

BEHIND THE THEORY

Edwin Hubble is famous for using redshifted light to show that the universe is expanding. However, the man who first measured redshifts was Vesto Slipher, who is largely forgotten. Slipher discovered redshift in 1912, at the Lowell Observatory in Flagstaff, Arizona. Percival Lowell had set up the observatory to look for Martians. He found none, but the observatory made many other discoveries. For example, Slipher hired Clyde Tombaugh in 1930, and the young researcher discovered Pluto soon after!

The James Webb Space Telescope (JWST) was launched in 2018 to study infrared emissions from early stars. Its mirror is seven times the size of the mirror of the HST, and is made from beryllium, a metal that will not distort if it gets hot. JSWT will always be in Earth's shadow, shielded from the sun's heat by a huge heat shield. The JSWT can see millions of light-years farther than HST and it can also make images of young stars forming inside dust clouds. However, it cannot see beyond the CMB into the Dark Ages. Is that even possible?

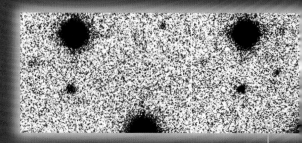

This image captured the oldest burst of gamma rays known, caused by an exploding star 12.8 billion light-years away.

GRAVITY WAVES

In 1916, Albert Einstein predicted that the gravity of all moving objects makes ripples in the fabric of space and time. Exactly 100 years later, a team of researchers detected these gravitational waves for the first time. The waves had come from two black holes colliding in deep space, making a very big splash in space-time. The waves were found by the gravitational wave detector, a complex system called the Laser Interferometer Gravitational-Wave Observatory (LIGO). LIGO showed that we did not need light or other radiation to image the universe.

LIGO is based in the United States, with a center in Louisiana and another in Washington State. It uses **lasers** to detect the stretching and squeezing of space-time caused by a passing gravitational wave. Both LIGO sites have two 2.5-mile (4 km) tunnels at right angles to each other. A powerful laser is fired into the start point, where it is split in half and sent down both tunnels. At the far end, a mirror reflects the lasers back to the start point.

What will gravity waves reveal about the structure of the universe?

UNANSWERED

One of the most exciting developments in space science is the Laser Interferometer Space Antenna, or LISA. LISA will use three satellites to beam lasers 1.5 million miles (2.5 million km) around the sun in a triangle. The lasers will detect waves passing through space. LISA will be so sensitive to tiny variations that it could search for black holes or dark matter—and perhaps see beyond the CMB to the very beginnings of the universe.

Scientists in the control room of LIGO look for evidence of gravity waves.

The position of the mirrors is finely adjusted, so one laser beam travels half a wavelength farther than the other. As a result, the lasers are out of sync when they return to the start point. When out-of-sync waves meet, they cancel each other out and disappear. If a gravity wave changes the length of a tunnel by even a tiny amount, the lasers do not cancel each other out but flicker instead. Scientists analyze the flickers to measure the waves, comparing the results from both LIGO sites. When they see the same patterns at the same time, they know the patterns were caused by a gravity wave.

Gravity waves are at the cutting-edge of space research. It might be many years before scientists figure how they affect our understanding of the universe. As often in the past, humans' desire to understand space is taking researchers far beyond the theory.

TIMELINE

1543   Nicolaus Copernicus shows that Earth and other planets orbit the sun.

1610   Galileo Galilei builds his own telescope and uses it to study the moon and Venus.

1680s   Isaac Newton proposes laws of motion that explain the structure and movement of the universe.

1780s   Pierre Laplace suggests the existence of "dark bodies" in space.

1845   Amateur astronomer Lord Rosse builds the Leviathan telescope and uses it to make the first images of distant spiral galaxies.

1908   Henrietta Swan Leavitt uses Cepheid variables to calculate the distance of stars from Earth.

1912   Vesto Slipher discovers redshift, the changing wavelength of light from stars moving away from Earth.

1916   Albert Einstein describes the workings of a "relativistic" universe in the General Theory of Relativity.

1927   George Lemaitre proposes a theory of the creation of the universe known as the Cosmic Egg. It later becomes known as the Big Bang Theory.

1929   US astronomer Edwin Hubble uses redshift to establish that other galaxies lie beyond the Milky Way.

1933   Fritz Zwicky uses the term "dark matter," though he has no theory about its nature.